Chapters

1. College: You ready or nah?

2. More Money, More Problems
   (Financing college)

3. No parents, No curfew, Big Problems

4. "The Freshman Fifteen"
   (First year peaks and valleys)

5. Oh sh!t, I fuc*** up…

6. Student Life

7. Sex, Drugs, Rock and Roll

8. Greek Life

9. Health, Wellness, Graduation, More?

About the Cover. About the Book

The Cover was created by Artist Justice Dwight Elder located in Richmond Va. He is my first cousin and a visionary with art the way that I attempt to be when I am writing. It was important that the cover portrayed a message that would entail many of the themes that will be in this book. For starters, I felt that it was important that the depiction of the graduates as children be shown. For me and many other black students, we are often prompted into this pipeline that ends with us as college graduates. At a young age, I was already being told "you are going to college". Partly because of society's structure of education. Partly because my parents wanted me to take the full advantage of opportunities that they may not have had themselves. Either way, it was engrained in me from childhood and I wanted to start there.

The depiction of blackness was also very important to me. I wanted to make sure that people knew who this guide was for and what this guide was about. I was not going to sugar coat blackness in effort to create more sales and reach larger demographics. Could I have written a guide that focused on college regardless of race, absolutely, but that simply would not be staying true to form with who I am and what my mission is. My mission is and has been to help black students have the knowledge and awareness of higher education and how that intersects with our cultural norms and lived experiences. I used traditional signs like the fist in the air and the afro to depict traditional symbols of blackness. It is important that even though we are going to college, which is a form of assimilation to society that we don't lose the core of who we are.

The book tells a story. Each chapter starts off with a story about myself based on the chapter and principles that I am discussing. The telling of my truth is necessary to lend value and truth to the tips, options, and hard hitting knowledge that I will be giving throughout the book. This isn't your ordinary college guide. We are going to be dealing with the real! Point blank and period. We are going to talk about drinking, sexual responsibility, gender, sexuality, academics, finances, and how all these things come together to create your intersectionality. The book uses a conversational tone with hopes of creating a connection to the words while allowing you to visualize what you are reading. The book will also cover topics that you wouldn't see in a typical college guide, but hey this is a book about what folks aren't usually telling you about college. Most importantly this book is about you. This book is about you finding out who you are, and how you navigate life through your collegiate experience.

You are not meant to live in pieces. This book will be used to reinforce the importance of living as a whole person.

Thank You

To all my family and friends who have been on this journey of self-discovery and enlightenment with me over the past 3 three years, I thank you. I didn't always know if what I was doing was right, but I did know that whatever it was I had your support and that has made all the difference.

Chapter 1

College: You Ready or Nah?

I can remember it like it was yesterday. It was the Fall of 2002 when I seriously started thinking about my future and what my plans would be after high school. I was sixteen, working a part-time job, learning how to drive and running track and field. I had been to all the sessions for the S.A.T., kept my G.P.A. above a 3.0 and knew that the time was nearing for me to make that big decision on where I would be heading that next fall.

The first question I asked myself was "am I ready for college?" We are often taught that college is the natural next step for us out of high school, however, for many of us, it isn't and will never be. Not everyone wants to go to college, and going without the motivation necessary to get a degree is the first step in setting you years behind on the next steps of your life. So, before you make that mistake, determine if college is the choice that you are making for you. Not your parents, or peer pressure, or society standards but for YOU!

Preparing for college should have honestly started your sophomore year of high school. So, if you are reading this guide now, then you are on the right track. However, if you are just getting this book and it is after your sophomore year, then it's time for you to get your mind together. There are several steps you need to be taking your junior and senior year to get you ready. Have no worries, because as the title state's this is "The _____ they don't teach you about college," so I will make sure you learn it now. We are going to step by step to make sure that you not only are prepared to go to college but have a resource guide that will get you through all four years (or more if you on that extended stay plan). So, let's get started with step 1!

Choosing a college

I thought that this process would be much easier but I didn't realize how many different school choices there were and the number of variables that go into making that choice. I remember getting mail daily from colleges across the country. All of them offering a different hope and dream that I should be following with them. I was quite overwhelmed back then as I was a first-generation student and didn't know exactly what I should be using to make my determination. I used things like location, major, accessibility, funding, programs, and asking others who had previously been to college during this process.

The next couple of sections will discuss the different options one has when looking for a college or university that will work best for them.

Public versus private

Publicly supported schools are generally state colleges or universities or two-year community colleges. These institutions receive most of their funding from the states in which they are located. Private schools generally have higher costs because they do not receive the same primary funding from the state and federal government.
Colleges and universities with religious affiliations are private. Most of them are Christian (Roman Catholic and Protestant), although there are a small number of Jewish and Islamic institutions. In most cases, you do not need to be a member of a church or religious group to attend a religiously affiliated college and enrollment in these

institutions will not usually interfere with your religious views.

Privately-owned Colleges (Peterson's)

Proprietary institutions are different from other types of schools in that they are privately owned and run for a profit. They are "educational businesses" that offer services and courses like those at other institutions, but you need to be very careful and research their accreditation status as part of your college search. Their programs tend to be technical and pre-professional courses of study.

Four Year Colleges

Four-year colleges and institutions are the traditional choice for most. They are typically set up to where you will do "general studies" in your first two years followed by two years of coursework in your major studies. These institutions can be specific to a degree, major area of study, and more, but will require four (or more) years of coursework before matriculation.

Two-year institutions

Which are typically referred to as community or junior colleges, award the associate degree — Associate of Arts (A.A.) or Associate of Science (A.S.) — following successful completion of a two-year, full-time program. A small number of two-year colleges offer the final two years of the undergraduate program only, awarding the bachelor's degree rather than the associate degree.

There are two basic types of programs at community and junior colleges, so you should have your career goals in mind when doing your college search.

Some programs are strictly academic and designed to prepare students to transfer to four-year institutions with bachelor's degree programs. Others are more practical or applied and provide career training in specific areas. This second type of school does not usually prepare students for transfer to a four-year institution, though some of the credits earned may still be accepted by a four-year institution.

Most community and junior colleges are publicly supported by the state and local communities, although some are private. Some private two-year colleges are proprietary or run for a profit. Investigate any college information you can find about these schools to get a better sense of their backgrounds.

PWI and HBCU

Every time I hear these two things come up I cringe and just want to run under a pillow and hide. Okay, so there are two main designations for schools in the United States based on the racial origins of the institution. PWI (Predominantly White Institution) and HBCU (Historically Black College or University). These designations were created many moons ago based on the make-up of the country during the time.

Let's start with PWI's. Naturally, when most colleges are absorbing the late 1700's and early 1800's, they were meant solely for white Americans as blacks were still considered property and slavery was very much alive and well. Over the years through segregation, integration, and affirmative action, we have seen the racial makeup of many of these institutions change to where they have a minority population on the campus and aren't referred to as PWI's as often because of this. As a black student, it is important to know the difference in the demographic make-up of the institution. This demographic change can be a complete culture shock for a student who may have never been to a school where they weren't in the majority population.

Now on to HBCU's. Per the White House HBCU Initiative, HBCU's are defined as HBCUs are a source of accomplishment and great pride for the African American community as well as the entire nation. The Higher Education Act of 1965, as amended, defines an HBCU as: "…any historically black college or university that was established prior to 1964, whose principal mission was, and is, the education of black Americans, and that is accredited by a nationally recognized accrediting agency or association determined by the Secretary [of Education] to be a reliable authority as to the quality of training offered or is, according to such an agency or association, making reasonable progress toward accreditation." HBCUs provide all students, regardless of race, an opportunity to develop their skills and talents. These institutions train young people who go on to serve domestically and internationally in the professions as entrepreneurs and in the public and private sectors. (White House Initiative on HBCU's)

When it was all said, and done for me, I ended up attending Virginia Union University, one of the oldest HBCU's in the south. It ended up being the perfect choice for me for several reasons. The first being that it was in Virginia and that I had family in the area on both my mom and dad's side. This created an environment where I had a home away from home. The school offered my major, well the major I had chosen at the time which was also a good thing. I was awarded a partial scholarship which ensured that I wouldn't have to come out of pocket for any expenses. The size of the school was also a good thing for me. The campus was small enough to walk from one end to the other in less than 15 minutes. This was a plus for me as this also meant that classroom sizes were small and I could build a personal connection with my professors.

Choosing the College

In the next chapter, I will go to financing college, so for now let's just stick to choosing the college. Once you have sifted through ALL the options that are available to you, you will finally be ready to make your selection. There is no right or wrong choice (unless you are going against what you want, then you are setting yourself up for an Epic Fail).

Visiting the Colleges

You will be a fool if you don't go and visit where you will spend the next 4 or more years of your life. I would be a rich man if I got money for each time a student dropped out and moved back home within the first four weeks of school because of homesickness, or simply just being unable to adjust to the environment. Visiting the schools is one of the most important things you can do before enrollment or even applying.

When you visit the campus, you should be looking for things that will interest you, the dorms, the area surrounding the campus, accessibility and anything else that you may personally prefer on the campus. Let's break this down some more.

Living Arrangements

Dorms are probably the biggest complaint I used to hear students talk about right after financial aid. The dorms are where you will be living for the next four years (unless you find outside campus housing which I will discuss later). It is important that you ask as many questions about the dorms to ensure that you have a comfortable stay. Here are some questions you should always ask.

1. Is living on campus mandatory freshman year?
   - There are still college campuses that make it mandatory to stay on campus during your freshman year and some for the first two years. You will want to inquire if your university has this requirement.

2. Are the dorms co-ed or single sex?
   - When you don't ask questions, you will end up with the short end of the stick. I have seen far too often parents not knowing that men would be in the dorms and vice versa cause grief for the students, parents, and the staff of the building. If you don't want to live in a co-ed dorm, make that known on your housing application and make sure that your parent or guardian is involved in that process.

3. Moving in and Moving out procedure
   - Some dorms allow for you to stay in the same room all year. Some only allow you to keep the same room for the semester and switch. Some

will allow you to keep your belongings in the room over the winter break while others require you to take your belongings with you. These are all the questions that you need to be asking. Again, the more you know up front, the less stress you will deal with on the back end.

4. Bathroom situation
    - The bathroom situation is the number 1 complaint once people get into the dorms. Some colleges have shared bathrooms per floor you on. Some have rooms that share a bathroom. Some have multiple shared bathrooms on the floor. It is important that you find out what type of bathroom situation your school has. If you are a person that is uncomfortable with sharing a bathroom with a lot of individuals, then dorm life may not be for you. Or you may need to inquire about other alternatives that the campus might have.

5. Amenities
    - All jokes aside, you better ask about the damn amenities. Don't get to school expecting you can watch TV in your room only to find out that they don't have cable. I see it happen too much. We are privileged in that many of us come from homes with our own bathroom or our own TV and bedroom. You aren't going to get that here, so I suggest you follow the "no question is a stupid question" and ask about the little things.

    - Do you have cable? Is there someone that cleans the bathrooms every day? Who do we call for emergency maintenance situations? Who do we contact if we are having issues with our roommates or other people in the dorm? Does each room have A/C and heat or is it a floor monitored thing?

6. What can I bring?
   - Not much more to say about this topic. Ask what you can bring. Don't be stupid and show up there with a bunch of shit that isn't allowed in the dorm. They will typically give you a list once you get to campus and sometimes before you getting there but be proactive and get that info up front.

7. Do you provide off-campus housing?
   - Some schools have off-campus apartment housing available. If you aren't too fond of the dorm life, ask if they have this option. Sometimes they can even use your financial aid to cover the expense if they have an arrangement with the outside apartment complex or they may own some themselves. It is always best to just ask.

8. Getting your roommate information
   - You will want to get to know your roommate before moving on campus. Once you decide that you will move on campus or into some housing, get to know who your roommate is going to be. Many times, roommates become your best friends in school, and it is important to build a bond before living with each with other.

After you have properly vetted all colleges that you are interested in for this information, you should be ok with making a final decision on where it is that you want to spend the next 4 (or more) years.

When in doubt about choosing a college, you must rely on what it is that you want. Again, you must make the best decision for you. This will be one of the most important decisions you will make in life.

Chapter 2: More Money, More Problems

I can remember my father's eyes getting big like quarters when we first started discussing the cost of attendance of various colleges I was looking at attending. Let me be clear when I say this, COLLEGE IS EXPENSIVE!!! Well, most of the time. The most important thing I learned during this process was that there is money out there if you look for it and know where to look. So, let's get started with the basics.

Financial Aid and Cost of Attendance

No two colleges are alike, and for that reason, the prices and fees are never alike as well. Deciding on the college you are going to attend goes hand in hand with looking at financing options to cover the cost of tuition, fees, room & board (meal plan) and any additional costs of living that may be incurred.

The "Cost of Attendance" is the first, and most often calculation you will hear regarding college financing. It is the cost per year of all tuition and fees that you are expected to pay to attend the college or university. That cost will range depending on several factors including the type of residency (in-state vs. out of state) and the type of housing (on or off campus). Once this has been determined, the next step is to contact the school's Student Accounts office to get the complete cost breakdown and summary. You can do this on your own. However, it is always best to let those with the expertise in this field conduct this part of the process, so you don't make any mistakes on the calculation.

Once you know the cost of attendance, it is time to have that very serious talk with parents, friends, family, etc. about how funding will work towards the cost of education. College is not cheap. College is a business, and like any business, they are in it to make a profit (or grow the endowment). However, their gain doesn't have to be your loss. With proper planning, you can set yourself up for success and not have the stress of worrying about affording college. With that said, let's talk about financing the cost of education and the various routes you have in doing so.

'Free Application for Federal Student Aid - FAFSA'

I remember completing my first FAFSA form. During that time it was still a paper application but was just starting to become electronic. It was a very complicated process with a lot of personal questions that my parents were nervous about answering. Let me tell you now that this form is not to be feared. Be as open and honest when filling it out online. Telling untruthful information will hold up your financial aid process.

As the official form used to request federal, state and school assistance in paying for college, The FAFSA asks questions to determine the student's level of financial need and establish his or her expected family contribution or the amount of money the student and parents are scheduled to pay out of pocket for the student's college expenses. The federal government, the colleges the student is applying to, and the states those colleges are in all use the FAFSA in determining how much financial aid to grant a student who applies for college financial aid. (Investopedia)

The application is used as a tool for colleges to determine what you might be eligible for regarding state and federal loans, grants, and scholarships. The application does require your parent/guardians tax returns (for dependent students) or your personal tax information if you are an independent student – (discussed later). The website uses an IRS data retrieval tool to pull the exact tax information needed to complete that application.

So FAFSA is where the magic starts. This application is free to use but does not always guarantee that you will receive free money. This application will explain your eligibility for loans in addition to certain grant funds.

Independent Student

> An independent student is one of the following: at least 24 years old, married, a graduate or professional student, a veteran, a member of the armed forces, an orphan, a ward of the court, or someone with legal dependents other than a spouse, an emancipated minor or someone who is homeless or at risk of becoming homeless. There will be additional information required to prove these requirements when you begin filling out the FAFSA.

Most people will be considered Dependent students so you will need your parents information to complete the online application.

The U.S. Department of Education has two federal student loan programs:

- The *William D. Ford Federal Direct Loan (Direct Loan) Program* is the largest federal student loan program. Under this program, the U.S. Department of Education is your *lender*. There are four types of Direct Loans available:
    - Direct Subsidized Loans are loans made to eligible undergraduate students who demonstrate *financial need* to help cover the costs of higher education at a college or career school.
    - Direct Unsubsidized Loans are loans made to eligible undergraduate, graduate, and professional students, but in this case, the student does not have to demonstrate financial need to be eligible for the loan. (Studentaid.ed.gov)

Loans made through the Federal Perkins Loan Program, often called Perkins Loans, are low-interest federal student loans for undergraduate and graduate students with exceptional financial need.

Here's a quick overview of Federal Perkins Loans:

- Available to undergraduate, graduate, and professional students with exceptional financial need.

- The interest rate for this loan is 5%.
- Not all schools participate in the Federal Perkins Loan Program. You should check with your school's financial aid office to see if your school participates.
- Your school is the lender; you will make your payments to the school that made your loan or your school's loan servicer.
- Funds depend on your financial need and the availability of funds at your college. (Studentaid.ed.gov)

Pell Grant

For most of us, these funds given by the government will not cover the entire cost of tuition. Federal funding is based on your FAFSA and the EFC (Expected Family Contribution) amount determined. The EFC is best stated as "what the federal government expects your family to be able to contribute to the cost of education". So, the higher the EFC, the less eligible you become for federal funds. The lower the EFC, the more federal programs like loans, grants, and work-study will be made available to you.

FAFSA can be submitted as early as January 1st of the year you will be entering in. It is important that you talk with your parents as their tax information will be needed to apply. The earlier you do your FAFSA and have it sent to the universities you think you may want to attend, the better chance you have of getting institutional funds from the school which I will talk about next. The good thing is that even if FAFSA can't cover your full cost of tuition; it is just a piece of the different types of funding that will be available to you.

INSTITUTIONAL FUNDS

Every college has institutional money or money that they can give you on behalf of the school. This money is usually directly tied to your GPA in high school or sports achievement. However, several schools have money available based on the major you choose. STEM (Science, Technology, Engineering, and Math} is a major program across the country that is aiming to place black students in these fields of study. Be sure that you are checking with schools once you choose your major to see if they have programs and funds available for students with a major.

Other institutional funds are called "endowed scholarships". These scholarships are set up by alumni and outside donors to help students who meet certain criteria based on the rules of the scholarship. This criterion can be based on race, gender, academics, major choice, and a variety of other things. These scholarships are sometimes given by the school automatically but you should inquire to the financial aid department to see if you qualify and where you can go to apply. Endowed scholarships are great because they don't have to be paid back and can be renewable as long as you keep up with the requirements being asked.

So, the most imperative reason that you get your FAFSA in as early as possible is that the school begins giving out their money on a first come first serve basis. So, those who take care of their financial obligations early (sending the FAFSA to the schools of their choice), are the ones who get better financial award packages.

Work Study

Every year I would apply for work study but never get it. I would be mad looking at all my friends pretending to have jobs on the campus but be doing nothing but gossiping lol. In all seriousness, the Federal work-study program is a great way to work and have the money go towards any unpaid balance on your student account.

This program helps students who still have a financial need based on FAFSA to be able to work a certain number of hours per semester in various departments across the campus. These funds can then either be given directly to the students or applied to the student account to help cover any balance owed to the university that might not be covered. This program is a great way to not only reduce the balance owed to the school but also gain work experience in a business atmosphere.

This program is not available to all students, however.

Outside Scholarships

I received several outside scholarships but I had to do some work to get them. I wrote essays to local and national organizations seeking funding for the additional expenses that are needed for school. Some of the scholarships went directly to the school while others came directly to me to be used for supplies and fees.

Scholarships are funds that don't have to be paid back. There are 1000's of organizations that give scholarships out every year based on certain criteria that you may qualify for. The problem with most scholarships is that people don't know where to look to make sure they are applying during the right timeframes. With Scholarships, I would suggest the approach of starting out local and then expanding further. So, check your city and local area organizations to see if they are giving out any type of scholarships. From there, I would then move to the state and nationwide organizations.

I always find it funny that people say "well google it, " but in the case of scholarships, there is nothing truer than this statement. If you already know what your major is, simply google "Scholarship available for students studying _____." See what comes up and begin applying. However, you should never be paying to find scholarships or to enter any scholarship database. **Anyone that is asking you to pay is nothing more than a scam!**

Also, make sure that you look at the historic black organizations that do this work. The United Negro College Fund is an excellent start to find free money. You create a profile based on the criteria being requested and instantly get entered in a database that will search for scholarships for you. In addition to this, you can actively search their database for scholarships that you can apply to outside of just filling out a profile. Make sure that whenever you are filling out scholarship paperwork that you are truthful with all answers they are requesting of you. There is truly no room for lying when applying for scholarships because you will be caught 99% of the time.

Many organizations out there are just like the UNCF and give funds to black students. Thurgood Marshall Foundation, Tom Joyner, Steve Harvey and more have scholarship foundations in place to help assist with the cost of college. It is important that you take the time and ownership over the research necessary to find these sources and make sure that you apply to them.

Award Letter

This will all go into what helps to create your "Award Letter." I stated it earlier, but I am going to go into a little more detail. The award letter will include ALL your financial aid (minus money from family and friends) to determine whether you have enough money to cover the cost of tuition and fees. You will get an award letter from every school you list on the FAFSA to have your financial information sent to.

The award letter will initially include all funding you receive through FAFSA, (loans, Pell grants). They will then add any state grants that you may be eligible for that the school may have to award out. They will then add any endowed scholarships that you may be qualified for as well. All the funding is added and then subtracted from the cost of tuition and fees to determine what you will owe or be owed. You can use that number to determine how much money you will need to raise out of pocket to cover those expenses.

Example

Stafford Sub Loan -	2,000.00
Stafford Unsub Loan -	3,500.00
Pell -	1,500.00
Outside Scholarship -	1,000.00
Endowed Scholarship -	1,500.00
Total -	9,500.00
Cost of Attendance -	- 10,000.00
Amount Owed -	$500.00

Momma and them...

Lmao. Let's be clear. Family and friends are also a source of finding some funding for college outside of the common traditional resources that most provide. The statement of a "closed mouths don't get fed" is so true when you need to lean on family and extended family to provide the resources needed for you to attend college. You cannot be afraid to ask for money to help with the cost of your future education. People are often willing to help especially if you make the one on one relationship with them so they can see how genuine you are about going to college. Ask everyone within your family circle for support as you take on this endeavor that will help set the next steps of your life in motion.

My best advice is to create a chart of people that you want to ask and then send out a letter asking for them to pledge funds towards your cause. With current technology, you can even set up a go fund me campaign to help monitor donors and ensure that everyone who has helped, you can get acknowledged in the process. Never go into asking for funding without a plan in place and making sure that you can sit and answer some tough questions around what you want to do in life. People don't mind investing in you, but only if they can see the return on investment.

Chapter 3: No parents, No rules, Big Problems

It was the summer before I went off to college when the rules first started to go away lol. I had graduated that June but school didn't start until August. Before that time, I had a curfew as most of us do in high school, but in preparation for college, the rules began to go out the window. That summer I got my first taste of freedom from my parents. I could hang out much later as long as I checked in, but I was still at home, so I felt they were still very much in control. However, that all changed that August.

I recall my first week of college being an interesting one. I had gotten an apartment right behind the school with my cousin, so I felt like an adult. I had to go grocery shopping, cook my food, wash my clothes, clean up and most importantly could come and go as I pleased.
Let me repeat; I could come and go as I pleased. The ultimate gift and curse for the 17-year-old who is now under no direct supervision.

I recall staying up EXTREMELY late that first couple of weeks at school. Not because I had to but just because I could. Those first couple of weeks in school I was just doing stupid shit because I finally could. My parents were 6 hours away, and I could give two fucks about what a consequence looked like. "I'm grown" became my response to everything those first few weeks until life kicked me in the ass and I realized that was some shit I had saw on TV and it was time for me to come back to reality.

The first weeks of college are going to be filled with a lot of transition and changes so let's get started with the basics.

REGISTRATION

Most schools have what is called a "pre-registration" period where you can avoid lines altogether. During this time, you can pay all your fees, set up a payment plan (if needed), and get cleared through the various offices and departments so that you can skip the entire first-day process and just check-in. This is always the best route because college can be very stressful the first couple of days, so the less stress, the better.

If you are behind schedule and are unable to pre-register, there is still a formal registration process for most schools that occurs during a freshman orientation week. The first day of registration, you always want to make sure that you have a parent or guardian with you because it can also be a stressful time, and administrators may want to ask questions that you might not be able to answer as the child. There can sometimes be paperwork that needs to be signed and additional fees that need to be paid as well so it is always good to have an adult be there who can navigate the conversation for full understanding.

My best advice would be to trust in the process. You are on the campus now so don't get so worked up and panicked that you are unable to be invested in the day fully. There may be long lines, and some confusion but don't let it get you down. Anytime you are feeling overwhelmed just take a moment to get a deep breath in and know that it is going to be okay. It is a new experience and with that comes the unknown. Even the most prepared can get hit with something "out of the blue" during this time so don't fret, just relax and go with the flow.

Moving in the dorm or apartment

Once you are through the registration process, it will be time to go into the dorm or some off-campus apartment living situation. Earlier I discussed all the questions you need to ask up front. Now it's time to move in. There will usually be dorm directors and student helpers there to help you move in on that day. If you make sure that you ask all the proper questions you need to upfront, this day should be very easy for you. Moving into the dorm or an apartment is usually the final step before your parents take off and you become an official "adult". You will also need to make sure that the campus doesn't have a curfew as some campuses close the gates and you could be in violation if coming in after hours.

The first few weeks of college are going to be very interesting. As I stated earlier, I was doing dumb things not because I didn't know right from wrong, or had a real purpose but simply because I could. If I could go back, there are a few things that I would have done differently to prepare myself for the adjustment into adulthood better.

1. A curfew

It's funny when you think of having a curfew when you are at home with your parents, but it makes a lot of sense as to why you might want to put one on yourself. When you are at home, you usually have someone responsible for getting you up in the morning and making sure you are prepared for school. College is not that place. If you are missing class, someone may contact you, or they may not. If you aren't turning in your homework and failing tests, no one is going to call mommy and daddy to give a progress report. So just as if you were still at home, I would advise that you set a curfew for yourself. Set a time where no matter what party or event or homework assignment, that you are in bed by a certain time. I will discuss it later, but time management is going to be critical to your success as a student.

2. Checking in

When I first went away, I didn't call home as often as I should have. Keeping the lines of communication open is important while away at school. I remember reporting back to my mother every time I got a good grade or my GPA increased, but that wasn't until my sophomore year when I did that. My freshman year I was trying to prove my adulthood and made every single mistake one could make along the way. Use your parents as a resource while in college. Don't be afraid to contact them when you make a mistake or misstep. It's a great sign of responsibility when you can tell your truth - good or bad.

3. Holding yourself accountable

I had to learn when I was first starting out in college. You must hold yourself responsible for what you are doing. Not everyone is out to get you. I can remember students telling me tales of "this professor did this" or "financial aid said that". I remember always having to give pushback to an administrator as to what it was they weren't telling me or weren't doing to ensure that these situations didn't keep happening.

You are now an "Adult," and in college, you will be treated like one. It is unfortunate that we believe that 17 and 18 make some switch go off that makes you more mature than the day before you went to college, however with proper planning you can ensure that you have a great start to your first year of college.

Chapter 4: The Freshman Fifteen

The "Freshman 15" is usually a term used to discuss the 15 (or more) pounds one would gain from stress, poor eating habits, and overall transition in life from being dependent to independent. In this chapter, however, I am choosing this to quickly discuss 15 things to expect during your first year of college. Many of these items will be expanded upon further in the book, but It needs to be said upfront, so you know what to expect.

1. Schedule and Classes
2. Academic Advisement
3. Midterms
4. Finals
5. Breaks (winter and summer)
6. Social Activities
7. Homecoming
8. Declaring a major
9. Diet
10. Friendships
11. Work/Life
12. Personal Finances
13. Relationship with Professors
14. Learning the Area
15. You made it through year one

1. Schedule and Classes

Don't mess this up lol. If you are not an early morning person, then you should not be taking early morning classes. Point blank and period! You have control over what classes you need to take (based on the curriculum of your major and list of options for year 1) and should make a schedule that is going to be conducive to the way that you learn. So, if you like to watch Maury or Court TV, don't schedule classes during those times that will force you to choose to be on time, or if you are the Father...

2. Academic Advisement

All schools will give you an advisor to help you navigate the classes that you need and more. Some schools will call them enrollment counselors, but their job is to make sure you are taking the necessary classes you will need on time to ensure a timely graduation. Make sure if you have questions that you ask them. If you don't like your class schedule or major, etc., these are the folks that you need to speak with to help you figure out next steps and make the best choice for you.

3. Midterms

In the middle of the semester, you will take a test that is called your "Midterms". This is how you will know that you are at the halfway point and is an excellent gauge of either how well you are doing, or if you will need to get your shit together to finish off the semester strong. IF you are struggling with your grades in some of the subjects, it is best first to talk to the professor about ways you can increase your grades. This may also be a good time to go to the academic center to get some tutoring help. Never be afraid to ask for help. You are in college, and you will not know everything.

4. Finals

At the end of each semester, you will take your Finals. Finals usually are comprehensive and cover all course work for the entire semester. Again, if your grades were struggling at Midterms, Finals are where you need to bring it all home. Finishing off strong not only builds confidence but can help improve your grades and GPA at the same time.

5. Breaks (Winter/Summer)

Schools will have break schedules that you will want to be acutely aware of. I had seen too many students end up stranded on campus, or kicked out of dorms because they did not properly pay attention to when it was time for them to leave. Also, leaving improperly during these breaks can lead to significant fines if you do not follow the proper checkout process. Going home for break is a great get away from the hustle and bustle of college so make sure you do it properly.

6. Social Activities

One of the best things about going to college is the new found social calendar that you will have if you so choose to get involved. College campuses always have weekly events, sessions, and programs being put on by student organizations and external agencies on an array of topics. The Student Life Office is the best place to find information on anything that will be happening on the campus. Making sure that you find things that you are interested in to attend and become a part of is important to the college experience. If you want to be involved in social activities and inspire your personal growth, making sure you are attending campus programming is going to be crucial in facilitating this.

7. Homecoming

The greatest party on earth. Lmao. No seriously, homecoming is one of the best weeks of college that occurs every year. It is the time when alumni can meet up with current students and share wisdom as well as reconnect after years of being apart. Homecoming is great because it gives you a lot of pride in your school and brings out so many people to make connections with. However, if you don't navigate homecoming correctly, you will become the story that everyone is talking about come Monday morning. For your first homecoming, try to take it all in. Go to the programs throughout the week, make sure you attend the football game and learn the lay of the land of your college campus. I will talk later about navigating partying, drinking, and other activities so for now, just try to make it to Monday, lol.

8. Declaring a Major

I will touch on this topic a few times throughout the book, but it is important that you declare a major or go listed as undecided. The good thing is you have time if you arrive at college and you don't have any idea as to what it is that you want to do. The first year or two will be general courses that you will need for any major that you choose. The important thing is that you are putting thought behind your major at some point so you can make the decision promptly. Again, when choosing a major you need to keep it about what you want and what your passions are. Not about what anyone else wants.

9. Diet and exercise

This is a hard one, but you must make sure you are taking care of yourself. Diet can be tough because there aren't always going to be healthy options available. Make sure you are eating three meals a day and not doing the 4th meal, Mickey D's and thanks before bed, and you should be okay. You can do simple things like running in the morning or some quick cardio before heading out to classes every day.

College brings about stress in a lot of areas, so you want to make sure your health isn't one of those things being overlooked in the process.

10. Friendships

College is the place where you will create lifelong friendships if you keep yourself open for the opportunity. I am currently friends with more people I went to college with than I am with high school or hometown friends. The people you meet in college become a second family. I remember being closed off to making friends initially because it was all so new to me and I didn't want to let anyone in really. Once I realized that I was only blocking myself from the opportunity to meet some great people I could open up to and create the relationships that I truly appreciate ten years later.

11. Work/Life

This is going to be another time management principle that you will want to make sure you get right. Work/Life balance will create your success or failure. Work doesn't always have to be a job either. Work can refer to the amount of time you give yourself for school work and studying. It is important that you put a decent amount of time to it, but you also are in college to grow the other aspects around your life. Life experiences are what college is all about. Vice Versa, making sure that you aren't getting too much "life" is just as important. A right balance between work and play is key to having a successful college tenure.

12. Personal Finances

Lmao. Okay, I had to laugh because college students are broke about 97.54% of the time. Being a broke college student is part of the deal in most cases. However, you can still manage your pennies. I had a job in college, so I did often have a few dollars in the bank to handle small bills and have some play money. Whatever money you do have, make sure you are spending it responsibly. So, if you know you will need books, make sure you are keeping money in reserve for that. Saving money aside for emergency situations is also going to be important. Check your bank account every day. Trying to keep a head count of your debit card spending is a poor practice that will leave you overwhelmed and OVERDRAFT!

13. Relationships with professors

Make sure that you make good working and professional relationships with you professors. Ten years later and I can still go to my alma mater and meet with my professors. It is important that you make sure they know who you are especially if you are struggling with their course. Professors are open to students that reach out for help opposed to those who complain about bad grades but never ask for help.

Also, NEVER MAKE EXCUSES TO YOUR PROFESSORS. Your professors have probably heard everything from "The Dog Ate my Homework" to "A dinosaur ate my homework". Seriously, the best policy when you are turning in something late or late to class is to be as honest as possible about what your situation is. Professors can smell bullshit a mile away, and if you are planning on giving it out, I hope you come prepared with boots and a shovel…

14. Learning the Area

My father always says to know your surroundings, know the entrance and most importantly know the exit. When moving away from home, it is imperative to know how to get through town and get to important places you may need in case of emergency. So, that means knowing where the local fire department, police department, and hospital is located. Knowing what areas of town you should be and shouldn't be at. Having mobile apps to ensure if you get stranded you can always get back to campus or home. Learning the area is as much about entertainment as it is about safety in your surroundings. One should never be scared to venture out but should also do it responsibly.

15. You made it through year 1

This can be short and sweet. You have made it through your freshman year of college. Now the real fun can begin. Once you feel your grades are stable, you can think about joining student organizations, frats and sororities, and getting into the other aspects of college. The next chapter is going to talk to those who may not have had the best of freshman years academically. However, even if you did well, the next chapter can help you not fall victim to a false sense of security.

Chapter 5: I F*cked Up But Survived

OMG! I have NEVER told this story, but I find it necessary to explain so that folk can understand that you can f*ck up and come back even stronger than before. Okay, let me get started.

The first semester I was a rock star. I got a 3.1 that semester and was well on my way to doing what I needed to do to get through my first year. Then I met the worst friend in the world, that took away my ability to think, but always made me think I had it all under control. Her name was Mary Jane lmao.

So, weed became my thing that 2nd semester and It took control over everything I had going on with college. at the time during the beginning of my second semester, I had several things going on. In addition to fighting with homesickness, I was working a part-time job, going to class, and dealing with paying my own bill for the first time in my life. The stress of these things led me to experiment with some recreational drinking and smoking. Drinking wasn't my thing yet, so it wasn't hard for me to stay away from that. smoking however was my thing, and I loved every part about it.

Wake and bake (waking up and hitting a blunt), in between the classes I could make, smoking at night and then making a crazy taco bell run had become the best part of my daily experience. While doing this, my grades were slipping hard and fast. I remember getting my midterms and having 3 F's and a C. Unfortunately, I was too high most of the time to even realize how bad this was and continued my trend of fucking up.

It wasn't until I realized that the people I was smoking with had no real ambitions or cares about their next steps in life that I learned that I had to get my shit together and fast. Luckily for me, my situation wasn't as dire as many of the other horror stories that I had heard about.

I lost my scholarship because my GPA dropped to a 2.8 and the requirement to keep it was a 3.0. I had also not passed enough classes to be classified as a Sophomore, so I knew that in year two I had a lot of work to be done. I went to financial aid and discussed my situation and could get some additional loan money to cover some of the shortfalls with my scholarship. I also picked up a job with more hours and better pay to help pay some of my tuition expenses. Although I was down, I was not out. That fight and determination were what I used to get me through that rough period and get focused on what I needed to do if I was going to graduate from college on time and on my own terms.

If you fall into this boat, it's going to be ok. Here are some steps you need to follow to make sure that you can get back on track.

Academic Probation

If your grades or GPA were abysmal than there are going to be some things that you need to do. I remember seeing some grades that were lower than an ant's ass to the ground. If your grades place you on academic probation, please make sure that you read the guidelines that will be sent out to you. They will stipulate how many credits you need to take as well as how many classes you need to pass to get back on track and off probation.

If your grades place you on an academic suspension, you must also read the guidelines to ensure that you follow the necessary steps to get off the suspension. Most schools will allow you to file what is call an "appeal" to get back into school without having to miss any time. Appeals are not guaranteed but should always be submitted anytime you are placed on this type of warning.

Being on academic suspension can also affect your financial aid. Making sure that you are following the proper steps to getting the suspension overturned and getting your financial aid restored are going to be key if you plan on finishing college on time. Messing up comes with life. The important thing is not to let life's mistakes become life's habits.

Financial Aid

During this process, you are also going to want to speak to several counselors at the school. A financial aid counselor to make sure that you are not on financial suspension. When you are on a financial aid suspension, there are several ways you can get your aid back, but it differs from school to school. You will need to make sure that you find out the process as it will have deadlines and requirements such as an essay, or interview around the circumstances of your case. In this scenario, you are not guaranteed to get your financial aid back, but it is important that you do everything you can to try.

Mental State

The most important thing is not to lose hope or give up and not to let it break you down mentally. You are going to have to be mentally strong through this process. It might make you angry or upset, but you must keep your temperament and chill and trust the process. Oh, and you also must have a conversation with your parents. Keeping them out of the loop is not a smart idea as they will inevitably find out.

College is all about survival lol. That's no lie. This chapter was short because I didn't want to mix my words when I tell you how to get back when you mess up. It happens. No one goes through college for multiple years unscathed. I graduated college on time with hard work after I messed up. You can also do the same.

Chapter 6: Student Life

Starting out on any college campus can be a daunting task to the freshman or sophomore. In addition to the culture shock, there as so many clubs and societies that are all vying for attention and memberships. Although I lived in an apartment right behind the school, because of the campus set-up, I was still heavily involved with campus activities.

I was a shy kid for the most part, so I didn't make myself known, but did make sure that I attended all the free events we had on campus. After barely making it through year 1, I had to get my ass back on track and did in a big way. This getting back on track involved me becoming more engaged in what was happening on campus.

Most colleges have Student Government Boards or Associations that have elections to help to create student leadership and development on the campus. This is a great first step to getting into campus involvement. Make sure you take some time out to research the different types of organizations that your campus has. I will talk about fraternities and sororities later, but this is more specific to other things on the campus you may want to be involved with.

Student Life as it's called will involve any and everything that your campus must offer to you outside of academics. This also includes the people you will meet along the way as you begin your journey and meet more and more students on the campus. So, I am going to discuss a few things around going into your major, but I am also going to give some key terms around sex, gender, and one that we all should know known as "Intersectionality."

Major classes Major Issues

It was the start of Junior year when the real fun began or the biggest fear of the rest of my college experience. The first two years of college are generally dedicated to your general studies. That is the 101's and 102's of courses such as English, math, history, and science as well as the general studies that will prepare you for your first set of major courses. I remember getting through my first two years with the ups and downs but being in a place where I was finally on track. However, it was now that I realized that the major I had chosen initially was not going to work for me.

I had been an Accounting major up until that point, but as I was going through my general studies and math courses, I realized that Accounting was not going to be something I could have fun with nor enjoy as my career path. The hard thing about choosing a major is that you feel like whatever you decide it will dictate how your life. I am telling you now, that you may get this decision wrong. As a young adult, it is hard making decisions like this and I wouldn't want you to think that you will get it right 100% of the time. What I will say however is that you can always fix this mistake to find your true path. I discussed earlier the importance in going into a field that you are passionate about. If you are led by your passion, you can never go wrong. It was at that time when setting up my schedule for my junior year that I decided to see my advisor to discuss the discourse I had with my current path and what steps could be taken to change my major.

This is the time to bounce ideas around to find out what major would best suit your needs. After about an hour of discussion, I changed my major from Accounting to

Finance. On paper that may seem small, but a little over ten years later I can see how big of a difference this one change made in my life. Once you choose your major, the next step is going through your major's classes until graduation. You should take some time out to review the coursework breakdown over the next few years to help make this decision.

Major classes have a much higher requirement than that of your general electives. Most schools require at least a B in your major classes to be considered as passing, in comparison to general elective courses. College is serious from day one, but it gets real once you are in your actual major. It is during this time that you will begin to learn the principles around your chosen course of study. It is also now when you need to decide on if this will be what you want to do moving forward. Very early on you will be able to tell if this is what you want to do so it is important that you get in tune with how you are feeling around your major. As you go through your major classes, they will get progressively harder and more intense as the courses progress.

During this time, you will also meet others who are in your program. The people who are in the same major as you are going to become resources on your journey through your final two years of college. Your major classes tend to be much smaller than that of the general electives because people are now going into their respective concentrations. Having a great relationship with your cohort mates in addition to the one you need to have with your major professors is key in having a successful academic experience.

Gender and Sex

I decided to include this in the book for several reasons, with the most important being that college will bring you into contact with people of different lived experiences and journeys. It is important that this is discussed before a person leaving for college as it could be complete culture shock to find out that there aren't only two genders and how people express themselves may not be something that you are used to. I'm going to start with the basics which are definitions of some key terms that one should know. It is important that as you attempt to understand others gender and sex identity, that you interrogate your own to ensure you are living life as you desire.

LGBTQIAP

Lesbian – People who identify as female, who are attracted to others who identify as female.

Gay – Although typically used when discussing men, the term is simply anyone who is attracted to the same sex.

Bisexuals – People who are attracted to both sexes, male and female. This is not a 50/50 thing and bisexuals can have a range of how their attractions fall across the scale.

Transgender - When a person is transgender it means that they are born a certain sex but identify as a different gender. (Someone at birth who is deemed male based on genitalia but identifies as a woman, or vice versa).

Queer - used as a very inclusive term for anyone in the LGBT+ community. Choosing to identify as 'queer' can mean individuals don't have to belong to a more specific category if they aren't sure of their sexuality/ gender or simply don't want any other label

Intersex - When someone is intersex it means they are born a certain gender but their sexual or reproductive anatomy is from the opposite sex. For example, someone who was born a woman might have genitalia that looks like a mix of both male and female genitalia... or it could be as unnoticeable as equally male and female chromosomes in their DNA.

Agender/Asexual - When a person is asexual it simply means that they aren't very sexually attracted to either sex and have a generally low level of interest and desire to take part in sexual activities.

Pansexual - When someone is pansexual it means they are attracted to people regardless of their gender. They are attracted to individuals rather than one gender or sexuality, and that can be whomever they fancy.

Heterosexual - romantic attraction, sexual attraction or sexual behavior between persons of the opposite sex or gender.

Cisgender - denoting or relating to a person whose self-identity conforms with the gender that corresponds to their biological sex; not transgender.

I know this can be a lot to take in but it is valuable information to not only know how others identity but investigate into self about how you may identify. Knowing that there are other genders and sexes that you may meet is only half the battle. The problem we have is this hierarchy of blackness created on how we identify. You can't be pro-black with conditions. Meaning a transgender black life is just as important as a heterosexual man's black life. Both deserving of respect, acceptance, equity, and equality.

The best advice I could give when you encounter someone of a gender or sexual identity that you may not understand is to have a conversation. Please know, that a person has a right to not disclose their sex, gender, or anything personal about themselves. However, if the person is willing, then be willing to listen and not judge. Again, I cannot say it enough; this is also the time you may want to investigate who you are and ensure you are the person you want to be, not the person you were told to be.

Intersectionality - is a term first coined in 1989 by American civil rights advocate and leading scholar of critical race **theory**, Kimberlé Williams Crenshaw. It is the study of overlapping or intersecting social identities and related systems of oppression, domination, or discrimination.

In a nutshell, it is how you take the different parts of yourself and how they come together to not only create your privilege but your oppression. So, for instance, being a man is a privilege in the eyes of society. However, being a black man creates a privilege and oppression as black men are more prone to be violent and treated a certain way based on these standards. It is important that we can realize how our privilege can take up space and when we need to utilize our privilege, vs. when we need to fight against our oppressions. The term is most often used when discussing black feminism but as a theory can be applied to the masses to discuss our lived experience.

Chapter 7: Sex, Drugs, Rock & Roll

Straight to the point, right? Well this isn't going to be quite as intense as you might think It will be, but it is necessary that you know the truth about the certain situation you may be placed in during your collegiate life. In addition to academics, college is also about social engagement and making connections that most take with them for the rest of their lives. With social engagement comes the exploration into the things that we were always told not to do. College is the place of self-discovery, self-discipline, and most importantly "every person for themselves!".

Sex happens. Sex is also something that you can be very much in control of. Having sex is, of course, a natural thing but still a subject that is very much taboo in our community. I can recall going to college as a virgin and being very afraid to navigate the discussion, let alone take it a step further to engaging in intercourse. Most important is the fact that you control your image and journey through this process. For men and women alike, sex is a taboo subject but one that will never go away. For that reason, let's talk about the importance around knowing your rights, your body, and how to navigate the sex conversation.

Sexual Assault and No Means No

As a college student, you are now looked at as an adult and will be treated as such throughout your college career. You will always be expected to make the "moral, ethical, and logical" decision that just a year ago your guardians would have been helping you to make. With that said, it is important that you are affirmed in who you are, know when a situation is not going the right way, how to exit and make sure that your safety comes first.

Sexual assault is a huge problem on college campuses across the country. We have seen time and time again where the policies surrounding it are archaic and poorly enforced which creates an environment conducive to this type of behavior. Rape is also a huge problem on campuses and in my opinion not properly investigated or swept under the rug in many cases. We even have cases where a person has plead guilty to these infractions and given less jail time than most traffic offenses.

Unfortunately, in this case, the narrative often (especially in cases of women making accusations) is treated with little support from school officials and the burden is placed on the victim rather than the offender. It is important that I emphasize that no one deserves to be sexually assaulted or raped. There is no type of clothing that should make you a target to having your body violated. People should have respect for who you are and your body regardless of age, race, clothing, sexual positivity and awareness.

Now let's talk about sex in general. You are going to be told several things about sex but the most enforced rule with being that "no one should be having sex on campus". So, I am going to advise you of the same. However, as adults who are sexual being we know that you are going to have sex. So rather than leave it at that, I am choosing to provide options and tips for when you make that decision.

Condoms

Condoms are still one of the most efficient preventative methods available to preventing Sti's (Sexually Transmitted Infections) and pregnancy. If you plan on having sex, make sure you are using a condom. Make sure that when you plan on going out, or on a date, or anywhere that you keep a condom on you. For the men, keep a condom on your person, but not in your wallet or in your car. The temperature could cause the condom to become defective. Also make sure that the expiration date is still good. For the women, you do the same with your wallet or bag. Sex is a natural part of life, but having a baby in college can affect your chances of graduating on time or being able to graduate at all. Remember what you are in college for, and keep that as your focus. Always be prepared however for consensual sexual encounters.

Oh. The pull-out method is not an option. No matter how much you may like condomless intercourse, the answer is no…

PrEP

Pre-exposure prophylaxis, or **PrEP**, is a way for people who do not have HIV but who are at substantial risk of getting it to prevent HIV infection by taking a pill every day. The pill (brand name Truvada) contains two medicines (tenofovir and emtricitabine) that are used in combination with other medicines to treat HIV. This may be an option for you if you are involved in what is considered high-risk sexual behaviors that may make you more susceptible to Std's.

STD/STI

Sexually Transmitted Diseases are now referred to as Sexually Transmitted Infections. They include but aren't limited to HIV, Herpes, Gonorrhea, Syphilis, Chlamydia, HPV, and HEP C. These are normal tests done during full panel testing. My advice is that if you are having sex regularly, then you need to be getting tested every 3 months. This is the best way to ensure that you are having a healthy sex life, and prevent any complications from untreated infections. I would also advise that if you are noticing anything like a discharge or burning that you go to your local doctor immediately for treatment. There is nothing to be ashamed about. Some STI's don't have side effects or show any signs which are why it is important to get the testing done as regularly as possible.

Sex involves consent as well. If you have not consented to sex than you need to report it to local school officials as well as local law enforcement officials. Do not be tricked into believing that you brought it upon yourself. Sex must be a consensual act.

Drugs

Lord. Forgive me as I tell all my truths. My first semester of college was amazing. I had made above a 3.0, went to all my classes, made some new friends and was fully involved in the college experience. It was during that first semester that I met up with some friends who I am still in contact with today. In addition to studying, "adulting," and working a part-time job, I also was also introduced to something that would change my entire life…

WEED!

LOL! Stay with me on this one. So, during the end of my first semester I began smoking weed with my new-found friends not often, but every occasionally. That occasionally then became very often and then daily. I can recall one day where we literally sat around trying to set a personal record of how much we could smoke in day. For the record that 13 blunts. The unfortunate side effect to this story was that while I was spending time being high all day, I wasn't keeping up with my responsibility in the classroom. I was becoming what is known as and "fiend" or a "weed head" and had totally lost focus of the goal that was ahead. Of course, I recovered and got my shit together, but I learned a valuable lesson and now I am going to give you some truth.

The opportunity to do drugs will be present when you go to college. It is truly for you to use willpower and logic not to engage in this. It is very easy to say "don't do drugs" however when you are in an environment that has this type of recreational activity going on, it is hard to resist the temptation, especially as a freshman when everyone is trying to get in where they fit and create a name for themselves. My best advice is going to be not to do it if you can. That is the best way to stay out of getting hooked and losing focus on your schoolwork.

Here comes the controversy. If you do decide that weed is your thing, then you need to be able to do it in moderation with the understanding and prioritization being on your school work and goals first. Why might I say such a thing? I say this because even after my 2nd semester slip up, I got back on track but I still smoked from time to time because I did enjoy it. I also know COUNTLESS college graduates who actively engage in weed and lead very productive and successful lives. This in no way serves as an endorsement for you to get hooked on weed, but I would not be doing my job if I didn't give it to you honest.

Let me also be clear when I say that weed is a gateway drug for a reason. A gateway drug can open the passage to using stronger drugs in the future. I do not in any way endorse drugs like cocaine, crack, molly, ecstasy, etc. Weed is bad enough if you get hooked and can't control it, so I would never advise you to do anything stronger. I also want to say that if weed is going to be your thing, that you should never be smoking with people that you don't know. Weed can be laced with many things and I have heard and witnessed horror stories around people smoking things that they don't know anything about and totally running their lives.

So, the best advice again is if you can abstain from doing weed, then refrain from doing weed.

If Weed is going to be your thing, it needs to be a controlled thing. Don't be late on bills but finding coins to get them dimes and nickel sacs. NO MAAM! This is not something that you should be going broke over, missing class over, or getting strung out on.

Don't let weed become your gateway to things much worse. Again, college is stressful and under stress we often do stupid things. You are in college for a reason. Never lose focus of that and you will be okay.

Rock & Roll

Okay so not exactly "rock and roll" cause we black folk more so like hip hop and R&B (But let's not forget that Rock and Roll were black first!) lol. So, when I speak about rock and roll, I am talking more about the party culture the will come with most colleges and the culture of the "college town" atmosphere.

So, I was very good at navigating the "Party and Bullshit" culture. I was in a fraternity so of course I loved a good party, especially the on-campus parties where you knew everyone who was in the room. I also participated in the throwing parties so I could see it from all angles, the sober and intoxicated. Partying is a great way to let loose after a week of classes, papers, exams, and whatever else was going on in the life of the average student. However, it is important that before you party, you plan and make sure that you never lose sight of why you are there.

I know and knew too many people that were all for the party but not for the academics. That is a huge mistake you could be making and one that you will need to check at the door. You are there to go to college. Everything else that comes with that can never trump the purpose that you are there for. I knew students and even some friends that made it to every party but were late on every paper, and even more nonexistent when it came to showing up to class on time. Partying can never the primary purpose of being in college.

So, this again is where we talk about that work/life balance. So, if partying is a part of what you want to do in college then you must make sure that you do it responsibly. That means putting a curfew on yourself especially if you have work due or class the very next day. I am going to talk about drinking next, but if you plan on drinking and partying don't plan on driving. Use a cab service or car app to ensure safety back to campus or your apartment.

Drinking

Some more controversy. Ok, so let me be clear when I say that I am not advising you to drink. Drinking underage is dangerous and drinking in general when you are of age can also be dangerous. So, I am going to tell you the best thing to do is to not drink. However, because it is college and I know the atmosphere, we know that drinking is going to happen. For that reason, if you are going to drink it is best to do so responsibly. Here are some things that you should think about if you are going to be drinking.

1. Never let anyone make your drink

IF you are at a party and plan on drinking there are two things you should do. The first is check what is in anything that you plan on drinking. The second is make your drink. People have been known to put things in a drink so don't be naïve thinking that everyone has your best intentions at heart.

2. Never go alone

It is always best to go out with a friend or a group of friends. Assign someone the designated driver or at least make sure that you can use a car mobile app to get you all home. Having a buddy system will help to protect you against yourself, and potentially from others. Make sure that you and your friends that you came there with are also the same one's that you are going home with. If you are not going back with your friends, be sure to let them know where you will be. My friends saved my life on several occasions. Having good friends that have your safety as their main concern is key.

3. Harm Reduction techniques

Harm reduction is the practice of doing things that reduce the amount of risk associated with a practice that may be harmful. If you plan on drinking, then it is important that you do your best to mitigate how much damage you are doing. So, try not taking shots or drinking straight up liquor with ice. This is a quick way to getting drunk fast and could lead to a disastrous evening. The next thing would be to make sure that you are using a mixer in your drink. Using juice helps to reduce the amount of alcohol intake per drink. Another thing you can do is to make sure that you are staying well hydrated throughout the night. I would advise that in between each drink that you have a cup of water. This way, in the span of time that you would've had four drinks you may have only had two drinks and 2 cups of water, again reducing risk.

4. Binge Drinking

Don't do it…

Seriously. Do not just keep knocking them back until you are knocked out unconscious. Binge drinking is dangerous and happens on too many college campuses with very tragic endings.

Recovery

Sometimes you may overdo it which will leave you with the dreaded hangover. Hangovers are the absolute worst. Over my lifetime I have had too many to count and as I get older, it gets harder and harder to recover from them. There are some tips though that can help you recover so that you can get back to your studies.

To help prevent a hangover, you should always make sure that you have had something to eat prior to drinking. Drinking on an empty stomach is the quickest route to having a bad night. Hangovers are most often caused by dehydration so making sure before you go to bed that you drink a good amount of water will help to keep you hydrated while you sleep. I also recommend my personal favorite, BC Powder. It is aspirin but crushed into powder form. It instantly hits your system and helps to remove the headache and the hangover. You can also google other home remedies and tricks to help you get through a hangover but these tips should work just fine.

Ohhhh, and if the room starts spinning at any point in the evening, you will need to find a bathroom or a bucket asap.

Chapter 8: Greek Life

I am very much involved in my brotherhood and the principles we stand for. I also understand the importance of sharing the knowledge to help the next group of members who seek to join our organizations because I was naïve. I didn't know anything about Greek life when I walked into it and could have messed up my chances because of that. So, I want to make sure that you have ALL (as much as I can give you) that you will need to help you along your way.

From School Daze to Drum Line, the depiction of Greek life in media was a for me while growing up in New Jersey. I remember entering college in 2003 and seeing all the different organizations on the campus. They were so confident and looked upon as the hierarchy on my HBCU campus. They were the leaders, the cool, kids, the "you can't sit with us" crew and I just had to be in it! It was the winter of 2005 and I had finally made my decision on what organization I wanted to join. I had been to a few programs and befriended a brother of the chapter from Detroit who also happened to be on the "Honda Campus All-Star Challenge" team with me. It was during the end of that semester that I finally gained enough courage to express my interest in joining Alpha Phi Alpha Fraternity Inc. I was advised to go the "interest meeting" and meet with the advisors to discuss my reasons for wanting to join and why I would make a good fit for the organization.

It would be in January that I would be notified by brothers that I had been chosen to become a part of the Gamma Chapter of Alpha Phi Alpha. Over the next few months I would attend programs, community service events all while being discreet about going through the National Process of Alpha. After fulfilling all my requirements of turning in my application and completing my National intake process, I was finally inducted as a member of Alpha Phi Alpha on March 25th, 2006. On April 7th, 2006, my line finally came out to the campus in a probate show to announce that we had completed the process of becoming members. That was and is still one of the best and most memorable days of my life. It was the first time that I truly came out of my shell and embarked on becoming the person that I am today.

As hard as it was to become a member, it is nothing in comparison to what it is once you become a member. You are obligated to do service, attend conferences, have deadlines and be accountable to not only yourself but to your chapter, organization, and the community that you serve. The "process" as many calls it, is minuscule regarding the work that you will do throughout your lifetime. 10 years in, I am still committed to the aims and motto of my organization and continue to do the work on various levels in the name of Alpha.

So, if you still want to become a member of a Greek Letter organization, continue reading. If not, you can go right on to the next chapter about partying lol. As stated before, Greek life is truly one of the most important decisions you will be making in your life. Being a member of a Black Greek Letter Organization, especially in the black community, has a long-standing history in the shaping of Civil Rights for African Americans since being established in 1906. These organizations are built upon the laurels of brotherhood and sisterhood in effort to bring about community through service projects based on Christian principles.

BGLO's have been established at hundreds of college campuses across the United States and have now begun establishing chapters as far as Europe and Africa. Combined, these organizations have inducted over 1 million members and continue to have a rich tradition and history in our communities.

So, let's start with the basics.

Fraternities:

There are 5 fraternities in the Divine Nine. Below is some quick information regarding these organizations.

Alpha Phi Alpha Fraternity Inc – Alpha Phi Alpha, the first intercollegiate Greek-letter fraternity established for African American Men, was founded at Cornell University in Ithaca, New York by seven college men who recognized the need for a strong bond of Brotherhood among African descendants in this country. The visionary founders, known as the "Jewels" of the fraternity, are Henry Arthur Callis, Charles Henry Chapman, Eugene Kinckle Jones, George Biddle Kelley, Nathaniel Allison Murray, Robert Harold Ogle, and Vertner Woodson Tandy.

The Fraternity initially served as a study and support group for minority students who faced racial prejudice, both educationally and socially, at Cornell. The Jewel founders and early leaders of the fraternity succeeded in laying a firm foundation for Alpha Phi Alpha's principles of scholarship, fellowship, good character, and the uplifting of humanity.

Omega Psi Phi Fraternity Inc. - is an international fraternity with over 750 undergraduate and graduate chapters. The fraternity was founded on November 17, 1911 by three Howard University juniors, Edgar Amos Love, Oscar James Cooper and Frank Coleman, and their faculty adviser, Dr. Ernest Everett Just. Omega Psi Phi is the first predominantly African-American fraternity to be founded at a historically black university.[1]

Since its founding in 1911, Omega Psi Phi's stated purpose has been to attract and build a strong and effective force of men dedicated to its Cardinal Principles of Manhood, scholarship, perseverance, and uplift. Throughout the world, many notable members are recognized as leaders in the arts, academics, athletics, entertainment, business, civil rights, education, government, and science fields.

Kappa Alpha Psi Fraternity Inc - is a collegiate Greek-letter fraternity with a predominantly African-American membership. Since the fraternity's founding on January 5, 1911 at Indiana University Bloomington, the fraternity has never limited membership based on color, creed or national origin. The fraternity has over 150,000 members with 721 undergraduate and alumni chapters in every state of the United States, and international chapters in the United Kingdom, Germany, Korea, Japan, United States Virgin Islands, Nigeria, and South Africa.

The fraternity was founded as Kappa Alpha Nu on the night of January 5, 1911, by ten African-American college students. The decision upon the name Kappa Alpha Nu may have been to honor the Alpha Kappa Nu club which began in 1903 on the Indiana University campus, but there were too few registrants to assure continuing organization. The organization is known today as Kappa Alpha Psi was nationally incorporated under the name of Kappa Alpha Nu on May 15, 1911 (the 1st nationally incorporated college fraternity by African Americans). The name of the organization was changed to its current name in 1915, shortly after its creation.

Phi Beta Sigma Fraternity Inc - is a social/service collegiate and professional fraternity founded at Howard University in Washington, D.C. on January 9, 1914, by three young African-American male students with nine other Howard students as charter members. The fraternity's founders, A. Langston Taylor, Leonard F. Morse, and Charles I. Brown, wanted to organize a Greek letter fraternity that would exemplify the ideals of *Brotherhood, Scholarship, and Service* while taking an inclusive perspective to serving the community as opposed to having an exclusive purpose. The fraternity exceeded the prevailing models of Black Greek-Letter fraternal organizations by being the first to establish alumni chapters, to establish youth mentoring clubs, to establish a federal credit union, to establish chapters in Africa, and establish a collegiate chapter outside of the United States, and is the only fraternity to hold a constitutional bond with a predominantly African-American sorority, Zeta Phi Beta (ZΦB), which was founded on January 16, 1920, at Howard University in Washington, D.C., through the efforts of members of Phi Beta Sigma Fraternity.

Iota Phi Theta - is a nationally incorporated, historically African-American, collegiate fraternity. It was founded on September 19, 1963 at Morgan State University (then Morgan State College) in Baltimore, Maryland. At present, it consists of over 70,000 members. There are currently over 300 undergraduate and alumni chapters, as well as colonies located in 40 US states, the District of Columbia, the Bahamas, Japan, South Korea and the Republic of Colombia.

The fraternity holds membership in the National Pan-Hellenic Council (NPHC), an umbrella organization comprising nine international historically African-American Greek letter sororities and fraternities, and the North-American Interfraternity Conference (NIC). The *Centaur* magazine is the official publication of the Iota Phi Theta Fraternity, Inc. First published as a newsletter, the *Centaur* has evolved into a biannual magazine.

Sororities:

Alpha Kappa Alpha Sorority, Inc.- (AKA) is the first Greek letter organization in the United States established by Black college women. Established January 15, 1908, at Howard University, the organization has now grown to a membership of over 170,000, with graduate and undergraduate chapters representing every state and several foreign countries.

Per the official web site, "Alpha Kappa Alpha is a sisterhood composed of women who have consciously chosen this affiliation as a means of self-fulfillment through volunteer service. Alpha Kappa Alpha cultivates and encourages high scholastic and ethical standards; promotes unity and friendship among college women; alleviates problems concerning girls and women; maintains a progressive interest in college life, and serves all mankind..."

Delta Sigma Theta Sorority - was founded on January 13, 1913 by twenty-two collegiate women at Howard University. These students wanted to use their collective strength to promote academic excellence and to aid persons in need. The first public act performed by the Delta Founders involved their participation in the Women's Suffrage March in Washington D.C., March 1913. Delta Sigma Theta was incorporated in 1930.

Per the official web site, "The Grand Chapter of Delta Sigma Theta Sorority, Inc. has a membership of over 200,000 predominately African-American, college-educated women. The Sorority currently has 900-plus chapters located in the United States, Tokyo, Japan, Okinawa, Japan, Germany, Bermuda, the Bahamas, Seoul, Korea, and St. Thomas and St Croix in the U.S. Virgin Islands." "blackgreek.com"

Zeta Phi Beta Sorority was founded on the simple belief that sorority elitism and socializing should not overshadow the real mission for progressive organizations - to address societal mores, ills, prejudices, poverty, and health concerns of the day. Founded January 16, 1920, Zeta began as an idea conceived by five coeds at Howard University in Washington D.C.

Per the official web site, "The purpose of Zeta Phi Beta Sorority is to foster the ideas of service, charity, scholarship, civil and cultural endeavors, sisterhood and finer womanhood. These ideals are reflected in the sorority's national program for which its members and auxiliary groups provide voluntary service to staff, community outreach programs, fund scholarships, support organized charities, and promote legislation for social and civic change."

Sigma Gamma Rho Sorority, Inc.- was organized on November 12, 1922, in Indianapolis, Indiana by seven school teachers. The group became an incorporated national collegiate sorority on December 30, 1929.

Per the official website, "Sigma Gamma Rho Sorority's aim is to enhance the quality of life within the community. Public service, leadership development, and education of youth are the hallmark of the organization's programs and activities. Sigma Gamma Rho addresses concerns that impact society educationally, civically, and economically."

The Fun Stuff:

This is what you see on TV. The stepping. The party-hopping aka "strolling". The Greek Picnic's. All of it. Honestly on the outside looking in it looks great. To be adorned by the yard and across the country while expressing our creativity through dance, step, and performance is something that I will always remember. What you don't see is the work that is put in prior. Every homecoming, practicing 3 to 4 nights a week for 8 weeks to prepare for a 10-minute show. Always needing to create new hops for competition and traveling whenever the newest song came out on the radio. The thing I learned about Greek life is that even the "fun stuff" was work. Nothing comes easy when you are upholding standards and principles of organizations with rich history and legacy doing the work for the black community. Here are some places you can look to gain so insight into the more social side of Greek Life.

YouTube:

You can easily Search YouTube for videos of each organization based on what it is that you are attempting to learn. Some of the videos will give historical data about the organizations and talk about the growth of the orgs over the past 100 years. These documentary style videos should be the first source that you use when making your decision on what org may be the best fit for you. It is important to know your history if you are ever going to know your future. So, before you get to do the "fun stuff," do your research! I will probably say this term ten more times, but it's because it is the most important misstep I see people make when inquiring about Greek life. The internet is full of history on the orgs so you would be putting yourself at a disadvantage to not seek the knowledge before expressing your interest.

After you have done your research, you can then use YouTube to get yourself pumped up for the flash and dash lol. I would start with Probates. So, the Probate is when new members of the organization introduce themselves to the campus. It usually involves a "show" inclusive of saying history in unison, performing greetings for other orgs and older frat and soror's, stepping, and introducing yourself to the campus. No two probates will ever be the same. However, it is important that you get a glimpse at one of the things that you will be working towards. Ten years ago, we didn't have the opportunity just to go online and see this. If you had never seen a probate before, you probably would not know what one would look like until you were on your own. I would take full advantage of seeing what you could potentially be getting yourself ready for.

Stepping and Strolling can also be easily found on YouTube. Stepping is a historical part of all organizations. You can view tons of footage on step shows over the past 30 years to see how intense, precise, and creative we can be when in competition with one another. Again, these are just small windows into what you may be signing up for so you should look at becoming Greek from every aspect possible.

Campus programming

Attending events on campus thrown by the various organization will also give you some insight into the social aspect of the organization as well as allowing you to see how they operate when running programming. From these events, you can get a feel of what the past and current members of the chapters are like to see if this is a group of individuals that you can mesh well with. Be certain, that you should never join or reject an organization based on the current members, but it is important to consider how you interact with them as they will be lifelong brothers and sisters to you.

Once you feel that you have done the proper research to decide, you must now begin the next phase of expressing interest. Discretion is key with any organization, as the principles and standards that we stand for are quite important. From the moment, you express interest, you will be judged on practically everything that you do. From your grades to your civic engagement, organizations are looking for the best quality members to help uplift the brand and continue to get the work done.

Interest Meeting/Rush:

Each organization will have what is called an interest meeting or for sororities a "Rush". You will need to look for postings throughout the campus or within the campus email system. If you are unsure you can always check with your student activities office to see programming for the organizations over the year. Business attire is required for this interaction as members from graduate and undergraduate chapters will be there to discuss information about joining the organization. This is the best place for you to ask any questions about the process moving forward regarding paperwork and any meetings. You will want to make sure that you are taking good notes as sign that you are dedicated to being timely and not to miss out on any important information.

Being a member of Alpha Phi Alpha for over 10 years, I don't take anything about it for granted. Greek life gave a person like me the opportunity to thrive and grow while networking and honing on my skill set to allow me to progress in life. I could do it all. I learned about brotherhood and friendship, professionalism, work/life balance, and created lifetime bonds with people who I am still in regular contact with until this day. For me, the fraternity gave and continued to give me a second place that I can call home and always go back to should I feel lost or in trouble. It is a strong part of who I am, and why I am and for that I am forever grateful. Remember that becoming Greek isn't just for show. This is truly a lifelong commitment that you are not only making to your organization, but to serve and uplift the black community. Make this decision wisely, as it will be one of the most important decisions you will make in life and help create your college experience, good bad or indifferent.

Greek life is not for everyone. Make sure if you are thinking about joining a Greek Letter organization that you again, do the research on the organization and on the chapter, that you are looking to join.

Chapter 9: Health, Wellness, Graduation, More?

Now that I am 31 I completely understand the importance of this, furthermore I understand how important it is that we are ensuring that our new 18-year-old adults also know the importance of staying healthy beyond diet and proper exercise. College isn't the best promotion of better eating at all. I think back at all the times I ended up sick in college and can directly relate it to the fact that I had poor self-care practices. If it wasn't emergency room necessary, I was going to class and to work. That is a problem. Our bodies have a way of telling us when we have reached our capacity and will completely shut down on us. I recall a time where it got so bad that my line brother literally forced me to go to the emergency room and come to find out that I had the flu. Had to stay out of classes for a week. On another occurrence, I let it get so bad that I had to go to the emergency room again and was diagnosed with pneumonia. These experiences have both made me think twice about choosing work over my health and my best advice would be for you to do the same thing.

Homesick: This is the first type of sickness I witnessed while working in administration at the university. During freshman year, dozens of students went back home simply because they were not properly prepared to go away to college. Within the first two weeks, we would have several students coming through our offices asking what the checkout process was as they were not fully prepared for all that college had to offer. No matter how much we attempted to talk them off the ledge, they had made up in their minds that they had just wanted to go home.

I'm not sure if there is any real remedy to stopping a person who gets homesick other than the importance of having a full understanding of what college life is like prior to arriving. I think that it is important for a student to know if you are ready to go to college, especially if you will be states away from home. It is imperative to have conversations with your parents about your feelings on being on your own. I also think it is a good thing to visit the school prior to attending and making sure you go to any orientations the school has so that you can meet other students before arrival.

Time Management:

If you don't manage your time well, you will stress yourself out and end up making yourself sick. You must make proper time for your classes, time for work, time for homework, time for studying, time for partying, and most importantly, time for YOURSELF! You are the most important person in your college journey, never forget that. Many times, we get caught up in what we are doing for our parents, or family, or community, and forget that we are also in college for ourselves. Make sure that you are making your time a priority, as you can't ever get it back.

Work Life Balance:

This goes hand in hand with time management. Many college students must work to afford to stay in college. However hard that may be, you must find time to decompress from work and enjoy life. If you are always working, you could be missing out on the important things that college must offer. Don't get so caught up with work that you miss the entire college experience.

I worked all four years of college, but I made sure that I had a schedule that was conducive to making sure I could enjoy college. This meant going on spring break, joining a fraternity, and being a part of a plethora of other organizations and programs that were occurring. I wouldn't have traded that experience for anything in world, and I wish that I took more time out to enjoy college instead of working as much as I did.

Managing Stress:

Never let anyone tell you that college students can't be stressed. I totally understand that parents and others may have bigger issues but that doesn't mean that what you are dealing with does not matter. The biggest thing to remember is that when you are dealing with stress, that you must acknowledge it when it is happening. I saw too many times where students simply flunked out due to poor management of their stress from work or school or a combination of several things. IF you are feeling stress, it is okay to talk to a school counselor about it. They are trained professionals who could help you with the management of what is going on in your life by creating a plan of action to help you deal with it. Also, remember as I stated before, to talk to your parents. People in college simply don't talk to their parents/guardians enough. If you can't talk to them, then you should talk to friend, whatever you do, try not to bottle it all in.

Graduation? More?

Senior year. I remember it like it was yesterday. Don't, however; I do remember it was a lot of work. Remember the story about me struggling during my first year? Well it came all the way back to bite me in the ass my senior year. By the time I got to it, I was 7 credits short. This meant instead of taking a full load of 17 credits each semester; I took 21 and 20 respectfully to graduate on time. I am glad that I did that. However, it was the hardest thing that I ever had to do.

Senior year is it. This is the time where you must make some tough decisions about the next steps in your life. Most think of this as the ending to a long journey, but this may just be the beginning. Nowadays, a bachelors' degree has become more and more common, which now has people seeking advanced degrees directly after coming out of undergrad. This is a decision that you will need to make based on the field of profession you are looking to get involved in. I remember waking up the next day after graduation and saying to myself "what do I do now?". You never want to end up there so senior year is as much about finishing as it is about preparing for the future.

Going back home or...

This is the first decision you must make. Are you going back home or staying where you are? I decided to stay in Richmond VA after I graduated from college for another six years. It was great for me to stay surrounded by my fraternity brothers, my friends, and keep in contact with many of the relationships I had built up. However, I have also known a lot of my friends to go back home right after school. It is a personal choice on what you think may be best for you. When you get to graduation, you are official "an adult"! lol. So, you now need to make some adult decisions that are in your best interest with the first being where you want to live. If you want to go home and then decide where you want to move that is fine. If you plan on staying in the same city, my best advice would be to move off campus during your senior year so that you can already be established once you graduate. If you get used to living on your own off campus, it will make the transition much easier once you graduate.

Graduate School:

I ended up going to grad school years after I had graduated and worked. For me it was better that I got some work experience under my belt before deciding to go back to school. This does not work for everyone, though. You must make the decision on whether you want to continue your education directly after college or take some time off to prevent overload and burnout. Some professions like medical school, lawyers, etc. require additional education, so it's a given for those on that path. For people in traditional degrees like business, English, science, etc. you must choose if going for further education is going to be for you. My best advice is that it's a personal choice and that grad school isn't for everyone.

It is now you will have the decision to make so don't take it lightly. As much as you want to breathe a sigh of relief that you have finished, I am here to tell you that you are just getting started. So, don't forget to think about next steps during your senior year.

The college experience is going to be different for everyone and I know that this book won't have all the answers. However, if you use some of these tips and stories to help navigate your own experience, I am certain that whatever blanks I may have missed, you will be able to fill in on your own.

Made in United States
North Haven, CT
17 May 2023